Film Studio Island 3

ACTIVITY BOOK

Contents

T0351731

Welcome

1  **Read and write *Jenny*, *John* or *Sam*. Then match.**

1 She's 9.
She's got black hair.
She likes pink.
Her name is ____Ruby.____

2 She's 11.
She's got red hair.
She likes films.
Her name is _____.

3 He's 8.
He's got blond hair.
He likes skateboards.
His name is _____.

4 He's 8.
He's got red hair.
He's got a sister.
His name is _____.

2  **Read and complete. Then draw yourself.**

I'm _____. I've _____ _____ hair.
I like _____.
My _____ _____ _____.

3   Look and write. Use the words in the box.

go home   go to school   go to bed
have dinner   ~~have breakfast~~   get up

Morning	Afternoon	Evening	Night
have breakfast			

4 1:11 Look and number. Then listen and check.

March ☐   September ☐   **June** ☐   *December* ☐

May ☐   **November** ☐   February ☐   **April** ☐

January ☐ 1   **August** ☐   October ☐   **July** ☐

5 1:12 Listen and circle.

13 ⃝30   14 40   **15 50**   16 60   **17 70**

18 80   **19 90**

6  Say a number from Activity 5. Ask your friend to point.

1 Free time

1 ✏️ Match.

cleaning

watching TV

playing football

skiing

reading

cooking

swimming

2 ✏️ Look and write.

1 I like ___watching TV.___
2 I like _____
3 I _____

4 I don't like ___cooking.___
5 I don't _____
6 I _____

3 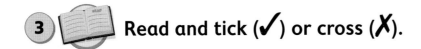 **Read and tick (✔) or cross (✗).**

Ruby likes cleaning and swimming. She doesn't like cooking.
She doesn't like playing football.
John likes cooking and playing football. He likes swimming.
He doesn't like cleaning.

4  **Look at Activity 3 and write.**

> **Yes, she does.   No, she doesn't.**
> **Yes, he does.   No, he doesn't.**

1 Does Ruby like cleaning?   <u>Yes, she does.</u>

2 Does John like swimming?   _____

3 Does Ruby like playing football?   _____

4 Does John like cooking?   _____

5 Does Ruby like swimming?   _____

6 Does John like cleaning?   _____

 **5** **Read and circle.**

1

I *like* / *don't like* skateboarding.

2

I *like* / *don't like* riding my scooter.

3

I *like* / *don't like* computer games.

4

I *like* / *don't like* playing the guitar.

 **6** **Read and tick (✔) or cross (✗). Then ask your friend.**

Do you like…?	Me	My friend
riding your bike		
skateboarding		
playing computer games		
riding your scooter		
playing the guitar		

 **7** **Look at Activity 6 and complete the sentences.**

I like _____

I don't like _____

My friend likes _____

He/She doesn't like _____

	skateboarding	swimming	watching TV	riding my bike
Me	✔			
My mum				
My dad				

9 **Look at Activity 8. Complete.**

like
don't like
likes
doesn't like

Hi, I'm Fiona.
I ¹ ___like___ skateboarding.
I ² _____ watching TV.

My mum ³ _____ skateboarding.
She ⁴ _____ watching TV.

My dad ⁵ _____ riding his bike but he ⁶ _____ swimming.

SOUNDS FUN!

10 1:21 **Listen and complete the words with *sk* or *sw*.**

1 <u>sk</u>iing

2 <u>sw</u>imming

3 __ateboarding

4 __ans

5 __ipping

6 __irt

7 __eets

11 Look and write.
Use the words in the box.

Madley Kool   Cleo the cat   cooking   pizza   sunglasses   ~~black~~

1 He's got short __black__ hair.

2 He likes wearing _____.

3 His favourite food is _____.

4 He doesn't like _____.

5 His best friend is _____.

6 His name is _____.

 **12** Look at the code and write the message.

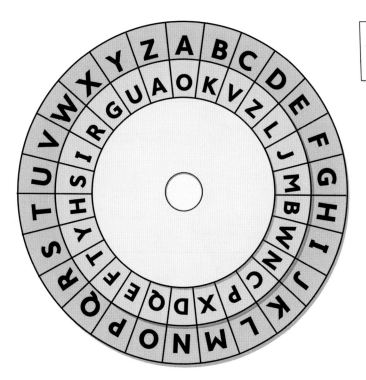

RBLTL WY XOZPLU CQQP?

W _____

_____

13  **Find out about Megan.**
Read and complete.

This is Megan.
She lives in a special
house. It's a castle.
Megan loves her
house. It's got
twenty-one rooms
and a big garden. She loves
playing in the garden and likes
reading outside. In the morning
she can hear the swans but at
night it's very quiet. She doesn't
like cleaning the castle, it's too big!

	Megan
house	
description	
birds	
likes	
doesn't like	

14 (1:24) **Listen and tick (✓).**

1

2

15 **Look at Activity 14. Read, think and write *1* or *2*.**

1 I like skateboarding. [2]

2 I don't like cleaning. [ ]

3 I like playing computer games. [ ]

4 I like reading. [ ]

5 I like playing the guitar. [ ]

6 I like watching TV. [ ]

16 Complete the puzzle.

Crossword:
- 1 (down): r e a d i n g
- 2 (across): s _ _ _ _ _ _ _ d i _ g
- 3: l a y
- 4: d
- 5: w i m m
- 6: e n n g
- 7: k n g

17 Read, think and complete.

Boy's list:
- cooking ✔
- reading ✔
- watching TV ✘
- playing football ✔
- riding my bike ✔

Girl's list:
- playing computer games ✔
- swimming ✔
- skiing ✘
- playing the guitar ✔
- skateboarding ✘

He likes ¹ __cooking__ and ² _____ . He likes ³ _____ football
and ⁴ _____ his ⁵ _____ . He doesn't like
⁶ _____ .

She ⁷ __likes__ playing computer games and swimming.
She ⁸ _____ playing the guitar. She ⁹ _____ skiing or
skateboarding.

18 What do you like doing?
Draw a picture.

I CAN DO IT!

19 What do you like doing? Use the words in the box.
Then tell your friend.

in the morning   in the afternoon   at night

_____

_____

What do you like doing in the morning?

I like books. I like reading in my bedroom.

Good   Excellent

2 Animals

1  Match.

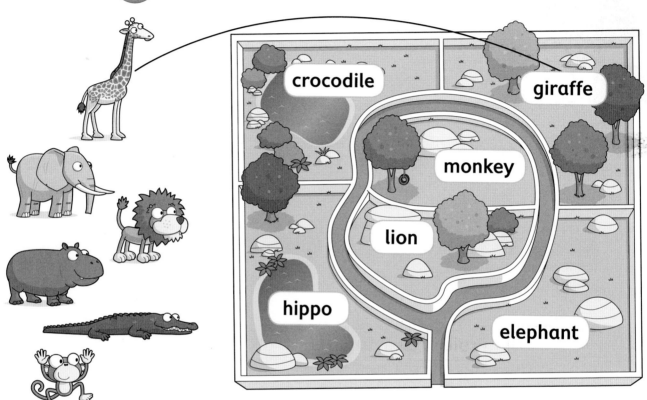

crocodile

giraffe

monkey

lion

hippo

elephant

2 Look and write.

1 _It's a lion._   **2** _It's an elephant._   **3** _____

4 _____   **5** _____   **6** _____

3  **Look and say *What do… eat?* Then write.**

| hippos ~~hippos~~ monkeys elephants crocodiles lions birds giraffes | eat | meat fruit insects leaves grass |

1 ___Hippos eat grass.___   4 _____

2 _____   5 _____

3 _____   6 _____

7 _____

4  **Look and write. Add two animals and complete. Then ask and answer.**

	Fruit	Leaves	Grass	Insects	Meat
monkeys	✓	✗	✗	✓	
lions	✗	✗	✗	✗	
elephants	✓	✓	✓	✗	
crocodiles	✗	✗	✗	✓	

1 Do monkeys eat fruit?
   ___Yes, they do.___

2 Do lions eat _____?
   _____

3 Do elephants eat insects?
   _____

4 Do _____ eat _____?
   _____

5 Read, think and circle.

1 Lions **(live)** / **lives** in Africa.
2 Oscar **live** / **lives** with me.
3 Lions **run** / **runs** very fast to catch their lunch.
4 Lions **eat** / **eats** meat.
5 Oscar **run** / **runs** very fast to get his lunch.
6 Oscar **eat** / **eats** meat.

6 Listen and number.

7 Look, think and complete.

1 Rabbits  __eat__ grass.

2 My dog _____ meat.

3 Monkeys _____ fruit.

4 My cat _____ meat.

5 Giraffes _____ leaves.

8 Listen and circle.

Monkeys

1 They live in **England** / **Africa**.
2 They're **big** / **small**.
3 They eat fruit, leaves and **insects** / **meat**.
4 They can **run** / **fly**.
5 They like **playing** / **sleeping**.

9 Find, think and write the questions.

1 (monkeys) (Where) (live) (do) _Where do monkeys live?_

2 (fruit) (eat) (they) (Do) _____

3 (run) (they) (Can) _____

4 (like) (What) (they) (do) (doing) _____

SOUNDS FUN!

10 Complete the words with *ee* or *ea*.
Then listen and check.

1 _e a_ ting 2 sixt_e e_n 3 l___ves 4 tr___ 5 thr___

6 j___ns 7 p___s 8 b___ns 9 m___t 10 sl___ping

11 (1:38) Listen and tick (✔) or cross (✗).

What animals are there in *Jim of the Jungle?*

12 Write the animals in the boxes. Add two more animals.

big

hippo

small

13 Look at the code on page 8 and write the message.

BL WYD'H WD HBL NSDMPL.

 **14** **Complete the crossword.**

1 Elephants say ____hello____ with their trunks
2 Elephants can't _____ .

3 Giraffes can _____ standing up.
4 Elephants can play _____ .
5 Giraffes have got long _____ tongues.
6 Giraffes don't _____ every day.

 **15** **Find out about an animal to complete the fact file.
Then tell your friend.**

An amazing animal	
Name	
They can…	
They can't…	
They've got…	
They eat…	
They like…	

16 ✏️ Find and write the words.

onil

ynekom

licordeco

popih

1 ___lion___

2 _____

3 _____

4 _____

17 ✏️ Write about monkeys. Use the words in the box.

~~fruit~~
trees
long tails
climb
ski

1 ___Monkeys eat fruit.___

2 _____

3 _____

4 _____

5 _____

Tell me about monkeys!

18 😜 Now ask and answer questions with your friend.

What do monkeys eat?

They eat fruit.

19 **Draw your favourite animal.**

20 **Write about your favourite animal.**
Then descibe it to your friend.

It lives in _____   It can _____

_____   _____

It eats _____   It likes _____

_____   _____

3 Weather

 **1** Match. Then say.

the sun

cloud

rain

snow

storm

wind

TODAY

 **2** Look, read and complete.

Here, ☀ ¹ _the sun_ is hot.

Here, there's a ☁ ² _____.

Here, there's a strong 🌳 ³ _____.

Here, there's a lot of 🌧 ⁴ _____ and

there's a big ☁ ⁵ _____ in the sky.

There's ❄ ⁶ _____ here today. It's cold.

3 🔘 1:45 **Listen and number. Then say.**

	1				

4 ✏️ **Look and write.**

> ~~wet~~ sunny cloudy snowy
> ~~rainy~~ stormy windy

1 It's _wet_ and _rainy_.

2 It's hot and _____.

3 It's _____.

4 It's _____. He's cold.

5 It's _____.

6 It's _____.

What's the weather like today?

It's _____. I'm _____.

5  **Look and write. Use the words in the box.**

~~spring~~   winter   autumn   summer

1 It's _____.

2 It's _____.

3 It's _____.

4 It's _spring._

6  **Look and write. Then match.**

snows   ~~rains~~   swim   fly
summer   autumn

1 It _rains_ in the spring.

2 The sun shines in the _____.

3 The wind blows in the_____.

4 It _____ in the winter.

I play in the snow.  ☐

☐ 1 I splash in the rain.

I _____ my kite. ☐

☐  I _____ in the sea.

7 1:48 **Listen and number.**

☐ ☐ ☐ 1

8  **Think and write the words.**

sunny ~~kite~~ ~~coat~~ ~~birds~~
hot   apples   snows
windy   strawberries
cold   rains   flowers

__sunny__
_____   ____

__kite__
_____

__coat__
_____
_____

__birds__
_____
_____

9 1:49 **Listen and complete the words with *ow* or *ou*.**

1 bl_o_ws

2 m_ou_se

3 sn___

4 rainb___

5 cl___d

6 tr___sers

7 h___se

10  Look and write.

1. It's cold.

2. _____

3. _____

4. _____

11 Read and complete. Use the words in the box.

cold   summer   ~~sun~~
sofa   hot

Cleo likes lying in the ¹_____sun._____ She likes the ²_____.
It's ³_____.
She likes the winter, too. The weather is ⁴_____ but Cleo likes lying on the ⁵_____.

12 Look at the code on page 8 and write the message.

VOD UQS YRWX?

13   **Read and circle.**
Then listen, check and write.

HURRICANE QUIZ

1 The centre of the hurricane is:
  A the heart.   **B** the eye.

2 In the centre of the hurricane:
  A it's windy. **B** it isn't windy.

3 There are hurricanes in the:
  A autumn and summer.
  B winter and spring.

1 The centre _____
2 In the centre _____
3 There are hurricanes _____

14 **Read and circle.**

TORNADO FACTS

Tornadoes are air tunnels. The air turns around very fast. They sometimes happen in the afternoon and in the spring and summer. There are a lot of tornadoes every year in North America. Tornado Alley is a place in the USA. There are a lot of tornadoes there.

1 The air _turns around_ / _jumps_.
2 You can see tornadoes in the _spring and winter_ / _summer and spring_.
3 There _are_ / _aren't_ a lot of tornadoes in North America.
4 Tornado Alley _is_ / _isn't_ in the USA.

15 Complete the crossword.

Across →

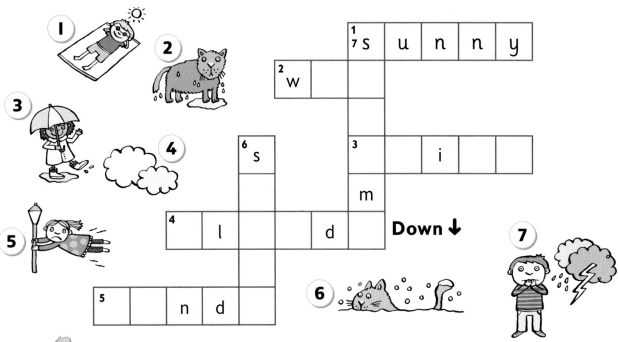

1

2

3

4

5

6

7

Down ↓

Across / Down grid:

1	S	u	n	n	y
2	w
3		i
6	s
	m
4		l		d
5			n	d

16 Read the email. Then complete the answer.

Hi! How are you? It's winter here and it's really cold. I love winter. It's my favourite season. I like skiing and playing in the snow with my friends. What's your favourite season? I don't like spring, sometimes there are tornadoes. I don't like rain but my little sister loves it, she jumps and splashes. She's only five.
Bye! :-)
Joe

Hi Joe,
It's ¹ __summer__ here and it's ² _____ . I ³ _____
the summer because I'm on holiday. In the summer I ⁴ _____
to the park and play ⁵ _____ with my friends. It's my
⁶ _____ season. I ⁷ _____ like autumn
because it's cold and windy. I've got a sister, too. She's thirteen.
Bye,
Claire

17 **Draw your favourite season.**

18  **Write about your favourite season. Then tell your friend.**

What is your favourite season?

My favourite season is _____

I like _____

I _____

Good   Excellent

4 My week

1 Look and write.

have Music lessons
go swimming
~~go skateboarding~~
have ballet lessons
do gymnastics
do karate

1   go skateboarding

2   _____

3   _____

4   _____

5   _____

6   _____

2 Look, think and complete.

go   have   do

What do you do on Saturdays?

1   I ___do___ gymnastics.

2   I _____ karate.

3   I _____ swimming.

4   I _____ skateboarding.

5   I _____ ballet lessons.

6   I _____ Music lessons.

3  **Listen and draw the times.**

4 **Look at Activity 3 and complete the sentences.**

| four o'clock   ~~ten o'clock~~   half past two   eleven o'clock |

1 Jenny does gymnastics at _____ten o'clock_____ .
2 Ruby has ballet lessons at _____ .
3 John goes swimming at _____ .
4 Sam goes skateboarding at _____ .

5 **Look at the diary and write.**

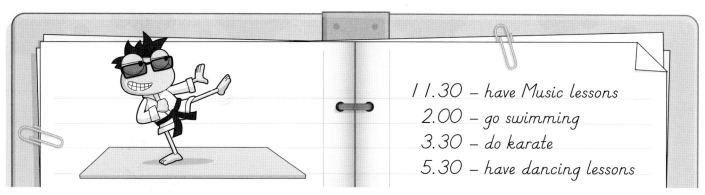

11.30 – have Music lessons
2.00 – go swimming
3.30 – do karate
5.30 – have dancing lessons

1 _____He has Music lessons at half past eleven._____
2 _____
3 _____
4 _____

6 How does he/she go to the park?
Look, think and write.

SONG

1 He goes by ___bike.___

2 She goes by _____.

3 She goes by _____.

4 He _____.

7 Follow and write.

1 He _____ goes to school by bike. _____
2 She _____
3 He _____

8 2:09 Listen and draw the times.

9 Find and write the sentences.

1 (lessons) (has) (Midge) (Music) (10 o'clock) (at)

Midge has Music lessons at 10 o'clock.

2 (does) (past) (half) (11) (She) (gymnastics) (at)

_____

3 (o'clock) (park) (2) (at) (She) (to) (goes) (the)

_____

4 (swimming) (at) (She) (4) (goes) (past) (half)

_____

SOUNDS FUN!

10 2:10 Think and circle the *z* sounds.
Then listen and check.

She say(s) she has short
Music lessons on Saturdays.

11 2:11 Listen and circle the words with the *z* sound.

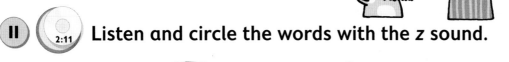

swimming (goes) tomatoes she does lessons
shorts has music carrots sofa potatoes

12 **2:13** Listen and match. Then write.

STORY

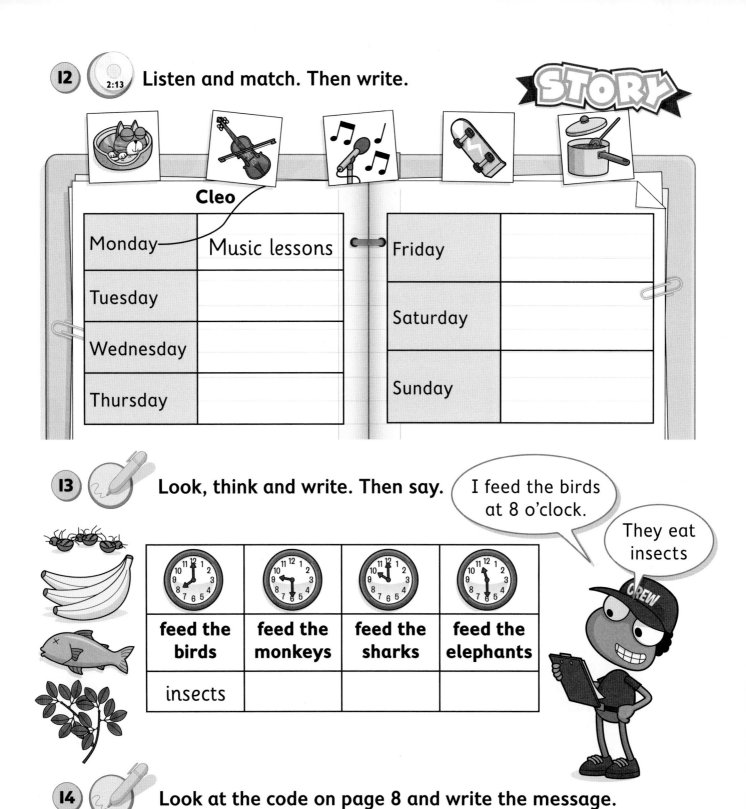

Cleo

Monday	Music lessons		Friday	
Tuesday			Saturday	
Wednesday				
Thursday			Sunday	

13 Look, think and write. Then say.

I feed the birds at 8 o'clock.

They eat insects

feed the birds	feed the monkeys	feed the sharks	feed the elephants
insects			

14 Look at the code on page 8 and write the message.

VOD XOZPLU CQQP YRWX?

15 🔊 2:15 **Listen and write. Then number.**

1 I __walk__ to school.

Alex

2 I go to school by_____.

Meiling

3 I go to school by_____.

Jodie

4 I go to school by_____.

Kabir

16 **Ask your friends** *How do you go to school?* **Then write.**

	by car	by bus	by bike	by boat	by train	walk
1 Me						
2						
3						

1 I _____

2 _____ goes _____

3 _____

17 Complete the words and find the answer.

1 I have balle t_ lessons.

2 I have M_ sic lessons.

3 I go skat_ boarding.

4 I go _ wimming.

5 I _ o kar_ te.

6 I do g_ mnastics.

What day is it? T_ _ _ _ _ _ _ _

18 Look at the diary and write about your day.

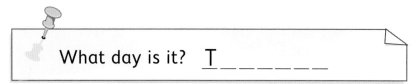

Monday

9 school (boat)	
11 karate (the park)	
2 swimming (a river)	
4 party	
8 home (plane)	

1 I go to school by boat at 9 o'clock.

2 _____

3 _____

4 _____

5 _____

19 What do you do on Saturdays?
Draw a picture.

morning

afternoon

20 Write about what you do on Saturdays. Then tell your friend.

On Saturdays, in the morning, I _____

_____

In the afternoon, I _____

_____

Good   Excellent

5 Jobs

1 Complete the words.   a e i o u

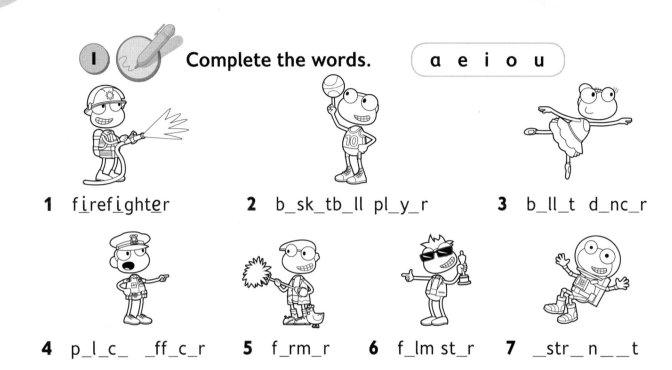

1 f<u>i</u>ref<u>igh</u>t<u>e</u>r

2 b_sk_tb_ll pl_y_r

3 b_ll_t d_nc_r

4 p_l_c_ _ff_c_r

5 f_rm_r

6 f_lm st_r

7 _str_n__t

2 Look and write.

1 I'm a basketball player.

2 I'm a _____.

3 I'm a _____.

4 I'm an _____.

5 I'm a _____.

3 🔊 2:23 **Listen and number. Complete the question.**

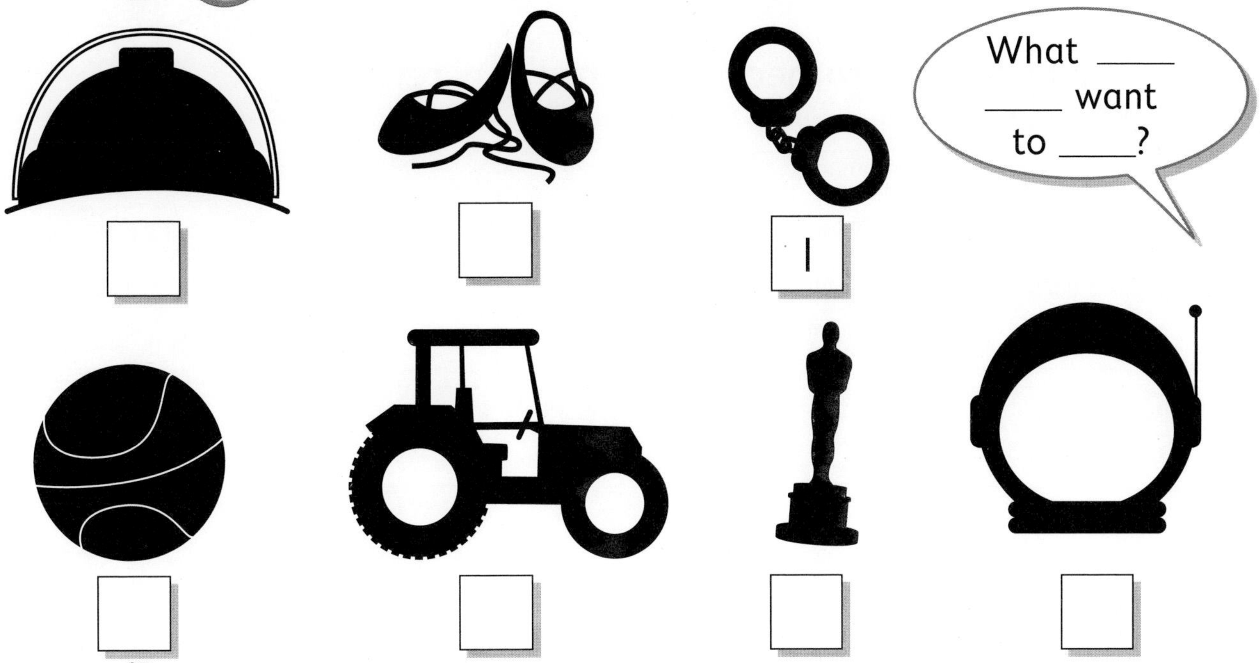

What _____ _____ want to _____?

☐   ☐ | 1 |

☐   ☐   ☐   ☐

4 **Look at Activity 3 and write.**

1   I want to be a police officer.

2 _____

3 _____

4 _____

5 _____

6 _____

7 _____

 **5** Find the jobs and write.

luberid   erathec   tocrod   refram

1

She wants to be a __doctor.__

2

He wants _____

3

He _____

4

_____

6 Find and write the questions. Then listen and write the answers.

1 (he) (want) (Does) (to) (a) (farmer) (be)

__Does he want to be a farmer?__   __No, he doesn't.__

2 (want) (be) (to) (teacher) (Does) (a) (she)

_____   _____

3 (a) (Does) (want) (be) (to) (he) (builder)

_____   _____

4 (doctor) (she) (want) (Does) (to) (a) (be)

_____   _____

7 Listen and tick (✓).

1 ✓

2

3

4

8  Look, think and write.

1   He's got a hat. He likes building.

He wants to be a builder.

_____

2

_____

3

_____

_____

9 Complete the words with *or*, *er* or *a*.
Then listen and check.

1 farm<u>er</u> 2 past__ 3 doct__ 4 banan__ 5 build__
6 sof__   7 pizz__   8 firefight__ 9 comput__ 10 wat__

10 Match.

STORY

film star

farmer

builder

1

2 doctor

3 firefighter

4

5

6

7 detective

teacher

11 Read and complete. Use the words in the box.

o'clock ~~farmer~~ tired morning
winter bed cows day

I want to be a ¹ _____farmer.____ I want
to have a lot of ² _____ . Farmers
get up at five ³ _____ in the
⁴ _____ . They have a very busy ⁵ _____ .
Then they go to ⁶ _____ at night. Phew! They're
⁷ _____ . It's good fun in the summer but it's
difficult in the ⁸ _____ .

12 Look at the code on page 8 and write the message.

RBOH ZQ UQS RODH HQ KL?

13 **Listen and circle.**

1 Hello, Matthew. What do you want to be?

I want to be a 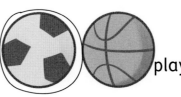 player.

2 What time do you go running in the morning?

I go running at .

3 What do you eat for lunch?

I eat .

4 What do you do after lunch?

I .

5 What do you do on Sundays?

I  with my friends.

14  **Look at Activity 13. Complete the article.**

playing   morning   ~~football~~   goes   plays   lunch

HE WANTS TO BE A CHAMPION!

Matthew wants to be a ¹___football___ player. He ²_____ running at 7 o'clock in the ³_____. He eats pasta and chicken for ⁴_____. After lunch he ⁵_____ football. He likes ⁶_____ computer games on Sundays.

15 Look and write.

1 police officer 2 _____

3 _____ 4 _____

5 _____ 6 _____

7 _____ 8 _____

9 _____ 10 _____

16 (2:33) Listen, read and find the differences. Listen again and write.

I don't like sport. I play basketball on Mondays at 11 o'clock. In the evening I go to the park with my friends. I want to be a film star and I want to be the best! My favourite player is Rajon Rondo. He's so cool! What do you want to do?

1 love 2 _____ 3 _____

4 _____ 5 _____

17 What do you want to be?
Draw a picture.

 **18** Write about what you want to be. Then tell your friend.

I like _____

I can _____

I want to be _____

6 Rainforest

1 Look and write.

rainforest waterfall river
mountain valley bridge

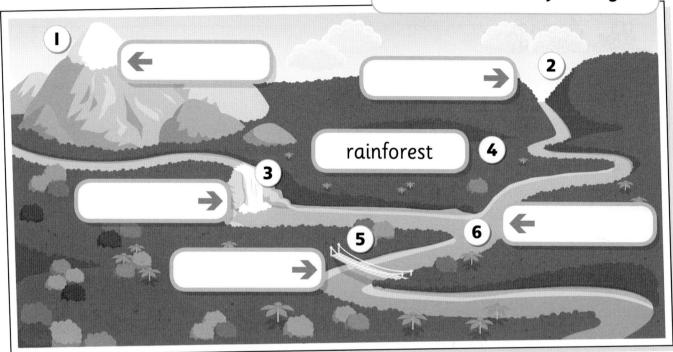

1
2
3
rainforest 4
5
6

2 Look, find and write the sentences.

1 | swimming | I'm | river | the | in |

I'm swimming in the river.

2 | mountain | a | climbing | I'm |

_____

3 | a | I'm | walking | on | bridge |

_____

4 | valley | a | walking | I'm | in |

_____

3 **Read, look and circle.**

1 The monkey is *next to* / *in* the tree.
2 The snake is *in front of* / *next to* the tree.
3 The frog is *next to* / *behind* the tree.
4 The giraffe is *under* / *behind* the tree.

4  **Look and write. Use the words in the box.**

> under   on   next to
> ~~in front of~~   behind

1 There's a cat _____ in front of the TV. _____
2 There's a football _____
3 There are skis _____
4 There's a crocodile _____
5 There's a hat _____

5   **Find and write the words.**

SONG

a sehwal

b mesokyn

c agelse

_____

_____

_____

6 2:40 **Look at Activity 5. Listen and number.**

7 **Read and complete.**

strong   eyes   tails
wings   ~~arms~~   sharp

Monkeys live in the rainforest.
They can climb trees. They've
got long ¹_____arms_____
and curly ²_____.

Eagles live in the mountains.
They can fly very high. They've
got ³_____ claws
and silent ⁴_____.

Whales live in the sea.
They can swim and they can sing.
They've got ⁵_____
tails and tiny ⁶_____.

8 (2:43) Listen and circle *True* or *False*.
What animal is it?

1	They live in the rainforest.	(True) / *False*
2	They can fly and run.	*True / False*
3	They've got short legs.	*True / False*
4	They've got strong jaws.	*True / False*

9  Read, think and complete.

	Hippos	Monkeys	Giraffes
live in valleys			
live in the rainforest			
live next to rivers	✓		
big jaws	✓		
long necks			
curly tails			

10  Look at Activity 9 and write.

Hippos _____ live next to rivers. They've got big jaws.
Monkeys _____
Giraffes _____

11 (2:44) Circle the silent letters.
Then listen and check.

1 balle(t)   **2** cupboard   **3** climb   **4** Wednesday
5 half   **6** know   **7** talk   **8** write

12 🎧 2:46 **Listen and write.**

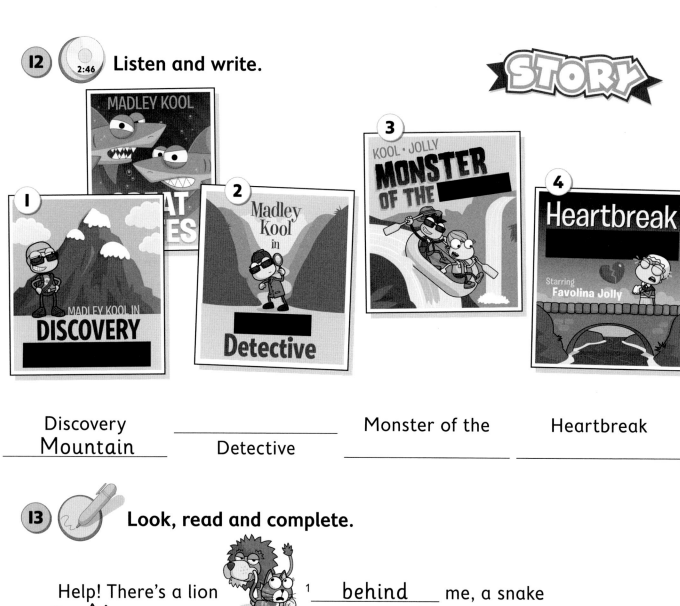

Discovery _____ Monster of the Heartbreak
Mountain   Detective   _____ _____

13 ✏️ **Look, read and complete.**

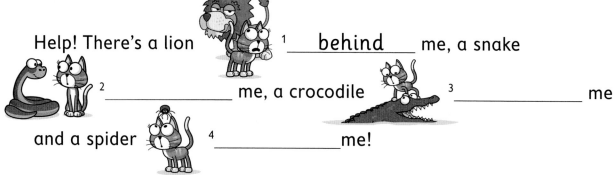

Help! There's a lion ¹ _____behind_____ me, a snake ² _____ me, a crocodile ³ _____ me and a spider ⁴ _____ me!

14 ✏️ **Look at the code on page 8 and write the message.**

ZQ UQS PWCL YEWZLTY?

15 **Look, think and complete.**

GEOGRAPHY

> eat tails ~~are~~ long
> live claws legs

These animals ¹_____are_____ big. They ²_____ in the mountains. They've got ³_____ necks and short ⁴_____. They've got sharp ⁵_____ and curly ⁶_____. They ⁷_____ leaves.

16 **Find, circle and write ten words from Unit 6.**

r	y	o	n	t	e	c	l	w	i
u	a	m	o	u	n	t	a	i	n
w	h	i	x	h	i	w	b	n	b
a	r	l	n	r	v	a	r	g	r
z	n	o	g	f	r	t	i	s	i
r	i	v	e	r	o	e	d	a	g
j	t	y	w	i	f	r	g	t	a
v	a	l	l	e	y	f	e	e	p
m	i	w	s	t	e	a	c	s	u
u	l	r	s	i	m	l	o	m	t
p	s	l	l	a	c	l	a	w	s
s	z	v	a	s	e	d	f	s	b

1 r ___ainforest___

2 m _____

3 w _____

4 b _____

5 v _____

6 r _____

7 t _____

8 w _____

9 j _____

10 c _____

17 Complete the crossword.

¹ r a i n f o r e s t

18 Look, think and write.

1 rainforest ___ They live in the rainforest.
2 long tails ___
3 sharp claws ___
4 fruit and insects ___
5 pretty ___

19  **Read and draw the animals.**

crocodile hummingbird hippo
spider snake monkey

I CAN DO IT!

20 **Write about your picture. Use the words in the box.
Then tell your friend.**

next to behind in front of under in on

1 The crocodile is _____

2 The hummingbird is _____

3 The hippo is _____

4 The spider is _____

5 The snake is _____

6 The monkey is _____

Good ☆ ☆ ☆ ☆ Excellent

7 Feelings

 Look and write.

tired   thirsty   angry   scared
sad   excited   ~~hungry~~   happy

 **1**  **2**  **3**  **4**

He's hungry. _____   _____   _____

 **5**  **6**  **7**  **8**

_____   _____   _____   _____

 Draw how you and your friend are feeling. Then write.

I'm _____

My friend _____

3  **Look and write. Use the words in the box.**

crying laughing ~~smiling~~
thirsty angry hungry

1 She's ___smiling.___
2 He's _____.
3 She's _____.

4 He's _____.
5 She's _____.
6 He's _____.

4  **Look at Activity 3. Read and match.**

1 Why is she smiling?   **a** Because he's hungry.
2 Why is he eating?   **b** Because it's funny.
3 Why is she drinking?   **c** Because she's happy.
4 Why is he shouting?   **d** Because he's sad.
5 Why is she laughing?   **e** Because she's thirsty.
6 Why is he crying?   **f** Because he's angry.

5 Read the answers and complete the questions. Use the words in the box.

cry excited laugh scared happy

1 What makes you feel ___excited___ ?   Parties.

2 What makes you feel _____ ?   Big storms.

3 What makes you feel _____ ?   Holidays.

4 What makes you _____ ?   Naughty monkeys.

5 What makes you _____ ?   Sad films.

6 Look, think and write.

1   They make me ___feel scared.___

2   They make me _____

3   They _____

4   They _____

5   They _____

7  3:08 Listen and tick (✔).

SKILLS

8 Read and match.

1 Rainy days make me feel sad   **a** because I love parks.

2 Parties makes me feel excited   **b** because I don't like rain.

3 Skateboarding makes me feel happy   **c** because they're fun.

4 Spiders make me feel scared   **d** because they're horrible.

SOUNDS FUN!

9 3:09 Listen and circle the correct picture.

1 bug   bag

 **2** hungry   angry

 **3** cut   cat

 4 cup   cap

 **5** Anna   Hannah

10 Read and match.

STORY

1 It's very big.

2 It's got a lot of teeth.

3 Its body is grey and white.

4 It eats fish but its favourite food is a seal.

5 It lives in the sea.

Food: fish, seals, turtles

Location:

Size: 5 metres ☐ | 1

Colours: black, grey or blue and white

Jaws: 300 teeth

11 Look, think and write.

Great White Shark

small fish   big fish   seal

Small ¹_____fish_____ are scared of ²_____ fish.
Seals are ³_____ of Great ⁴_____ Sharks.
Big ⁵_____ are scared of ⁶_____.

12 Look at the code on page 8 and write the message.

W OX DQH YVOTLZ QJ YBOTCY.

13 **Read and circle.**

It makes me feel *happy* / *scared*.

It makes me *cry* / *laugh*.

It makes me feel *sad* / *happy*.

It makes me feel *sad* / *scared*.

14  **Listen and write.** 3:12

1 It makes me feel sad.
2 _____
3 _____
4 _____

15  Look and circle. Draw and write the one that is missing.

otthirstysuscaredmlangryczexcitedahtiredwihungry

 _____

16 Look, think and write.

Why?
~~shouting~~ crying
smiling laughing

Because
funny ~~angry~~
sad happy

1 Why __is she shouting?__
Because ____she's angry.____

2 Why _____
Because it's _____

3 Why _____
Because _____

4 Why _____
Because _____

17 ✏️ **What makes you feel happy and scared? Draw pictures.**

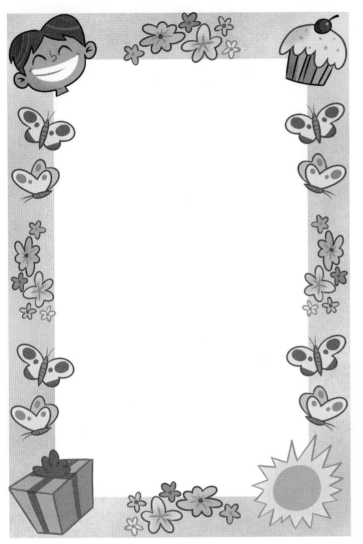

18 💬 **Write about your pictures. Then tell your friend.**

_____ me feel happy.

_____ me feel scared.

Good ⭐ ⭐ ⭐ ⭐ Excellent

8 By the sea

1 ✏ Match.

surfing

horse-riding

fishing

snorkelling

sailing

2 ✏ Look and complete.

Jenny is ¹ ___sailing.___ Sam is
² _____, John is
³ _____ and Ruby is
⁴ _____. Cleo is on the
⁵ _____.

Jenny is ⁶ ___fishing.___
Sam is ⁷ _____, John is
⁸ _____ and Ruby is
⁹ _____. Cleo is in the
¹⁰ _____.

3  **Look, read and complete.**

1 What's she ___doing?___
She's ___watching TV.___

2 What's she _____
She's _____

3 What's he _____
He's _____

4 What's _____
He's _____

5 _____
She's _____

6 _____
_____

4  **Look, think and write.**

What do you like? What are you scared of?

| sharks | the sea | horses | crocodiles | storms | doctors |

I like   I don't like   I'm scared of

_____   _____   _____

_____   _____   _____

_____   _____   _____

| bored with | keen on | scared of | terrified of |

sunny   walking   watching   ~~raining~~   plays tennis   drinking   bus

Lucy is  ¹ __bored with__ the weather. It's

² __raining.__ She likes ³ _____ weather because

she's ⁴ _____ tennis. She ⁵ _____

on Tuesdays. Today is Tuesday but it's raining.

Lucy is ⁶ _____ to the tennis club. She doesn't

go by ⁷ _____ because she's ⁸ _____

buses. ZAP! A storm! Lucy is ⁹ _____ storms.

Poor Lucy!

Lucy is home again. She's ¹⁰ _____ TV and she's

¹¹ _____ some hot chocolate. She's happy. But

there's a spider in the living room. Oh dear! Lucy is

¹² _____ spiders. This isn't a very good day!

6 **3:23** **Listen and complete the postcard.**

SKILLS

Dear Mum and Dad,

I'm having fun here in the ¹ <u>mountains</u>.

There are a lot of things to do. Every morning I go

² _____. It makes me feel ³ _____

because I ⁴ _____ horses. I like ⁵ _____

but today it's ⁶ _____ and I'm writing postcards

in the hotel. William is ⁷ _____ of climbing!

He likes ⁸ _____ in the river. I'm not keen on

the river. Are there crocodiles here?

See you soon.

Lots of love,

Emily

Mr and Mrs ⁹ _____

32 ¹⁰ _____ Road

Norwich

NR3 ¹¹ _____

7 **Write a postcard in your notebook.**

SOUNDS FUN!

8 **3:24** **Complete the words with *or* or *ur*.**
Then listen and check.

1 h<u>or</u>se   **2** s<u>ur</u>fing   **3** n___se   **4** sn___kelling   **5** st___m

6 t___n   **7** m___ning   **8** sh___rt

Listen and circle.

1 Madley Kool says he is **an actor** / **a film star**.
2 His favourite film **is** / **isn't** Great Whites.
3 Madley Kool is **scared** / **terrified** of sharks.
4 There **are** / **aren't** sharks in his next film.

  Read and complete.

film	making	acting	saves
people	sharks	man	~~film star~~

INTERVIEW WITH
MADLEY KOOL

Madley Kool is a great [1] __film star__ !
He likes [2] _____ adventure films.
His new [3] _____ is Great Whites.
In this film, there are some big
[4] _____. Madley Kool is a brave
[5] _____ in the film and he
[6] _____ a lot of [7] _____.
In real life, Madley Kool is scared of sharks.
But he's a good actor. He says, 'I like
[8] _____ but sharks are scary.'

 **Look at the code on page 8 and write the message.**

W RODH HQ BOIL YRWXXWDM PLYYQDY.

12 **Complete the word maps with animals.**

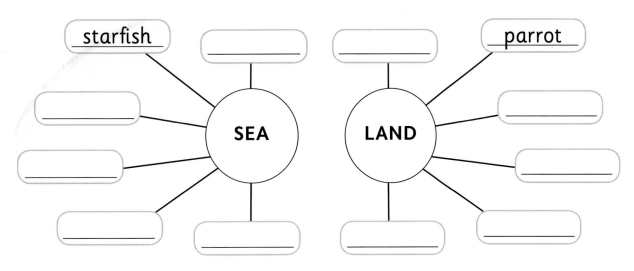

starfish | SEA | | parrot
LAND

13  **Read. Then match.**

PENGUINS

Adélie Penguins live in Antarctica. They live on the land and in the sea. They eat a lot of fish. In the winter they go swimming a lot because it's very cold on land. They can swim but they can't fly. The penguins are black, white and red. They've got long tails and they live for twenty years.

1	Do they live in Antarctica?	**a**	No, they aren't.
2	Do they eat fish?	**b**	Yes, they have.
3	Can they swim?	**c**	Yes, they can.
4	Can they fly?	**d**	Yes, they do.
5	Are they black and pink?	**e**	No, they can't.
6	Have they got long tails?	**f**	Yes, they do.

14 Find the odd one out.

1 ~~insect~~   cleaning   reading   skiing

2 lion   crocodile   cry   hippo

3 Tuesday   November   Friday   Sunday

4 scared   snowy   wet   rainy

5 astronaut   beach   basketball player   builder

6 river   waterfall   plane   rainforest

7 horse-riding   sailing   fishing   winter

15 Read and complete. Use the words in the box.

ballet dancer   skateboarding   of   ~~autumn~~   by
like   and   morning   terrified   Saturday   past

Hi, I'm Elizabeth. My favourite season is ¹ __autumn__
and I love the pretty colours. The leaves on the trees
are orange ² _____ red. I ³ _____
horse-riding. I'm not scared ⁴ _____ horses
but I am ⁵ _____ of spiders! I love my horse.
I like ballet, too. I want to be a ⁶ _____.
I have lessons on Mondays and Saturdays at school.
My lessons start at half ⁷ _____ eight in the
⁸ _____. It's very early!
I go ⁹ _____ bike because it isn't far away.
On ¹⁰ _____ afternoons I go to the park
and go ¹¹ _____ with my friends.

16 What do you like doing on holiday?
Draw a picture.

I CAN DO IT!

17  Write about what you like doing on holiday.
Then tell your friend.

On holiday I like _____

_____

Good   Excellent

Christmas

1  **Read and match.**

1 Grace opens her presents in
    a the morning.
    b the afternoon.

2 She eats a special
    a breakfast.
    b lunch.

3 She eats turkey and
    a sprouts.
    b rice.

4 In Christmas crackers there are
    a puddings.
    b jokes.

5 Grace plays with her brother
    a in the garden.
    b in her bedroom.

2 **Look, think and write.**

1 He likes ___swimming.___

2 She likes _____

3 _____

4 _____

5 _____

Mother's Day

1  **Look at the chart and complete the sentences.**

Country	Month
Italy	May
Kenya	June
Argentina	October
Russia	November

1 In <u>Italy</u>, Mother's Day is in May.

2 In Russia, Mother's Day is in _____.

3 In _____, Mother's Day is in June.

4 In Argentina, Mother's Day is in _____.

5 In my country, Mother's Day is in _____.

2  **Draw, colour and write a Mother's Day card.**

Have a lovely
Mother's Day!

Happy
Mother's Day!

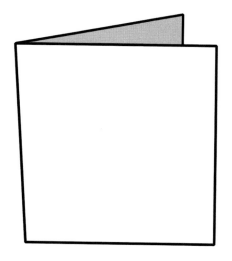

I love you, Mum!

Thanks for everything!

Thank you, Mum!

Picture dictionary

Free time

 swimming

 playing football

 cleaning

 reading

 skiing

 cooking

 watching TV

 riding my bike

 playing the guitar

 skateboarding

 playing computer games

Animals

 elephant

 lion

 monkey

 giraffe

 crocodile

 hippo

 insects

 fruit

 grass

 meat

 leaves

Weather and seasons

 spring

 summer

 autumn

 winter

 cold

 hot

 the sun / sunny

 cloud / cloudy

 snow / snowy

 rain / rainy

 storm / stormy

 wind / windy

 wet

My week

get up

go to bed

go skateboarding

go swimming

go to school

go to the park

go to a party

do karate

do gymnastics

have ballet lessons

have Music lessons

Jobs

firefighter

police officer

film star

farmer

ballet dancer

basketball player

astronaut

teacher

builder

doctor

The natural world

waterfall

mountain

rainforest

river

bridge

valley

sea

eagle

whale

Feelings

tired

thirsty

hungry

angry

scared

excited

happy

sad

smiling

laughing

crying

shouting

By the sea

sailing

surfing

snorkelling

horse-riding

fishing

beach

coral reef

Christmas

turkey

pudding

cracker

snowman

snowball

Mother's Day

card

box of
chocolates

tea

toast

rose